- EASY PIANO -

CHRIS TOMLIN
see the morning

ISBN-13: 978-1-4234-2681-3
ISBN-10: 1-4234-2681-9

HAL•LEONARD®
CORPORATION
7777 W. BLUEMOUND RD. P.O. BOX 13819 MILWAUKEE, WI 53213

Visit Hal Leonard Online at
www.halleonard.com

www.christomlin.com

CONTENTS

HOW CAN I KEEP FROM SINGING

Words and Music by CHRIS TOMLIN,
MATT REDMAN and ED CASH

There is an end - less
lift my

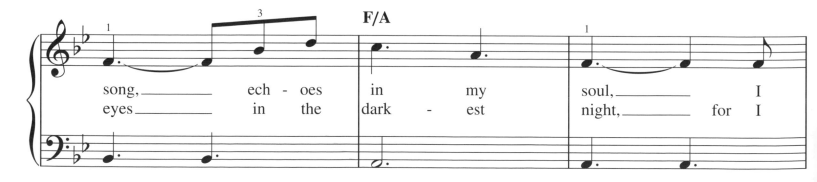

song,_____ ech - oes in my soul,_____ I
eyes_____ in the dark - est night,_____ for I

5

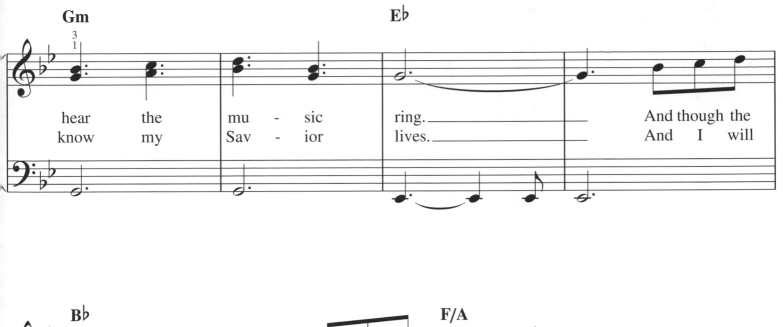

hear the mu - sic ring._____ And though the
know my Sav - ior lives._____ And I will

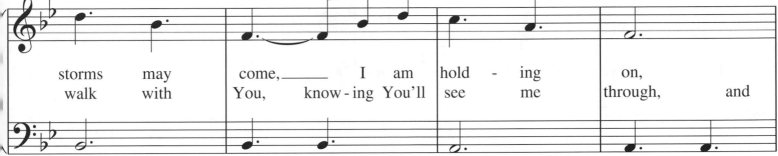

storms may come,_____ I am hold - ing on,
walk with You, know-ing You'll see me through, and

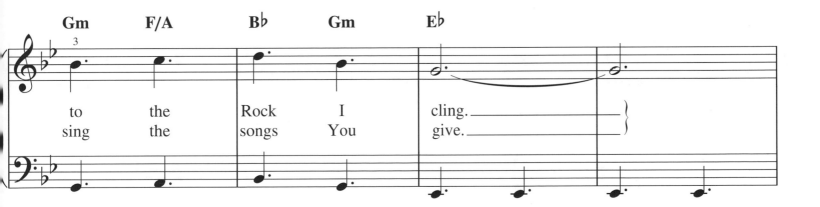

to the Rock I cling._____
sing the songs You give._____

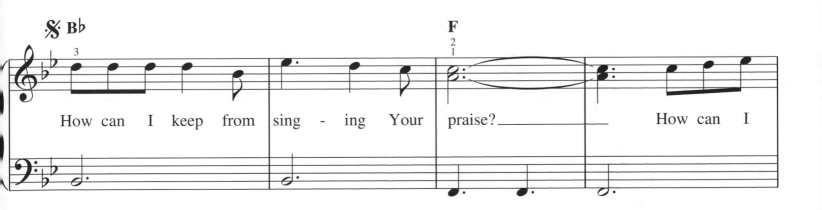

How can I keep from sing - ing Your praise?_____ How can I

ev - er say e - nough,____ how a - maz - ing is Your love?

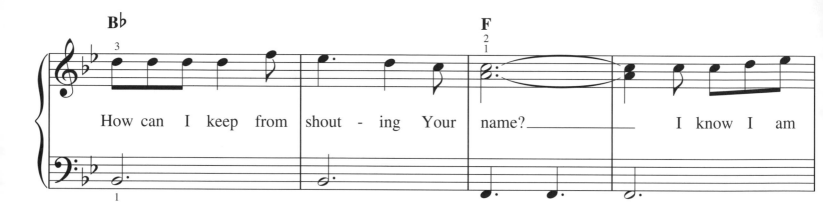

How can I keep from shout - ing Your name?____ I know I am

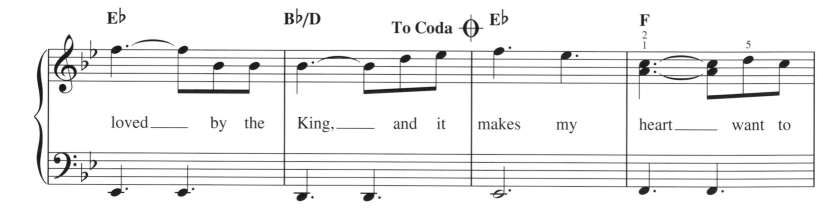

loved____ by the King,____ and it makes my heart____ want to

sing. I will

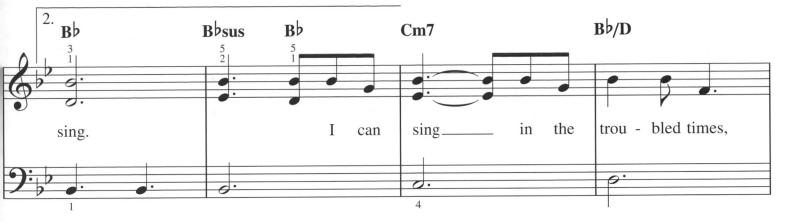

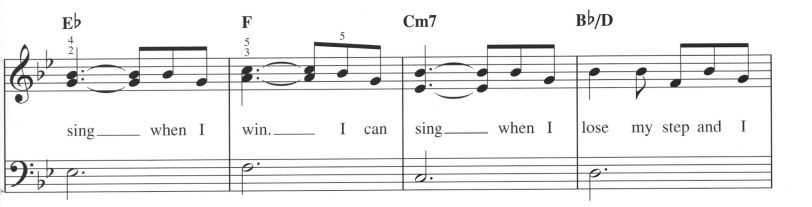

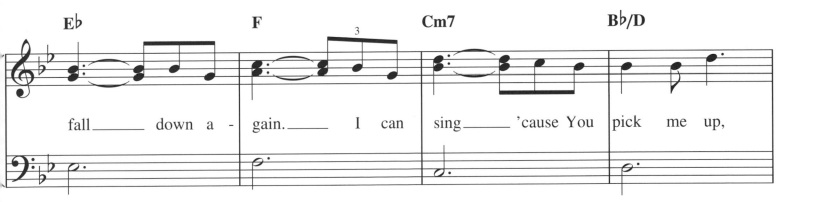

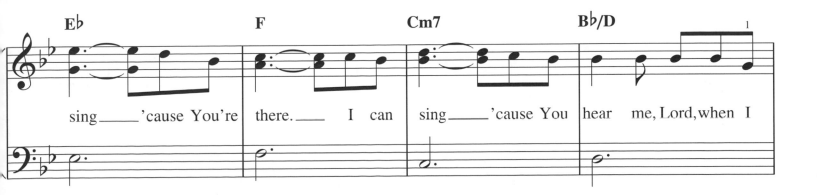

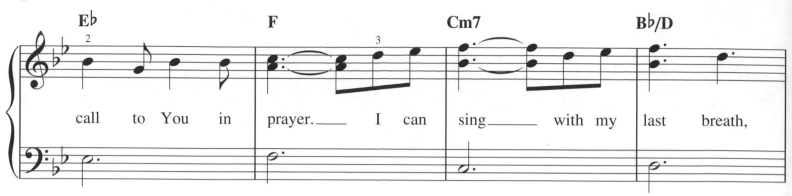

call   to   You   in   prayer.____   I   can   sing____   with   my   last   breath,

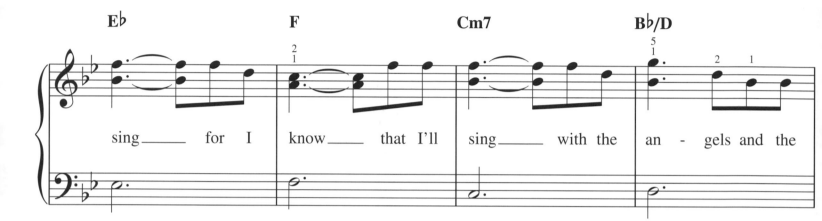

sing____   for   I   know____   that   I'll   sing____   with   the   an - gels   and   the

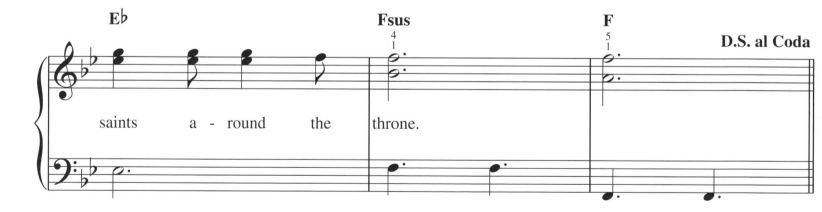

saints   a - round   the   throne.

D.S. al Coda

CODA

makes   my   heart...____   I   am   loved____   by   the   King,____   and   it

makes my heart... I am loved by the King, and it

makes my heart want to sing.

MADE TO WORSHIP

Words and Music by CHRIS TOMLIN,
ED CASH and STEPHAN SHARP

Moderately

Be -

fore the day,____ be - fore the light,____ be -
All we are___ and all we have__ is

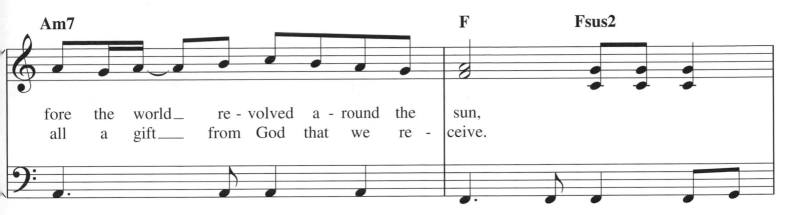

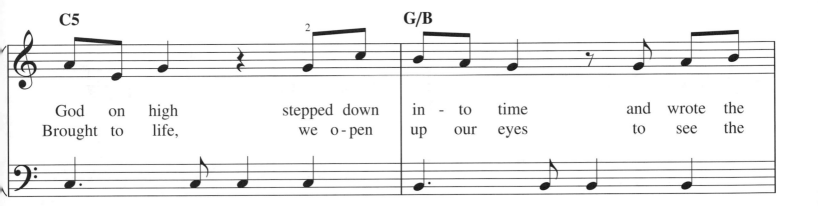

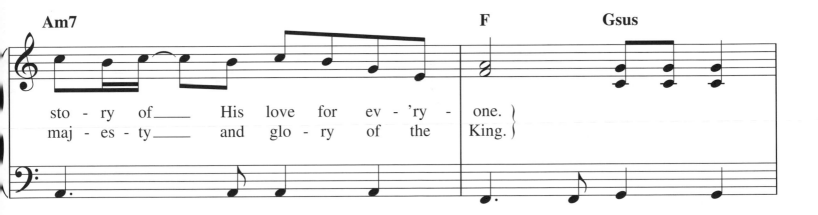

12

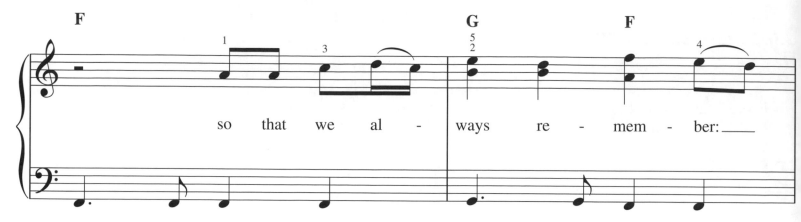

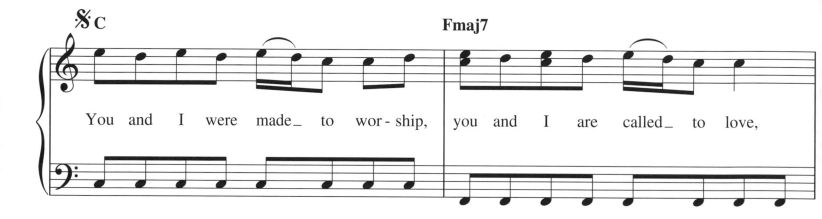

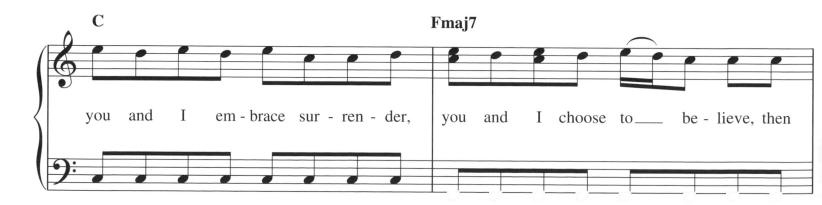

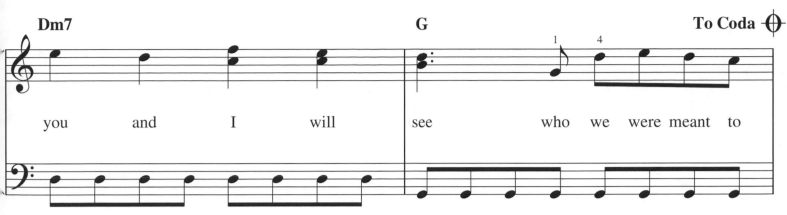

Dm7

G

To Coda ⊕

you   and   I   will   see   who   we   were meant   to

1.

C5

be.

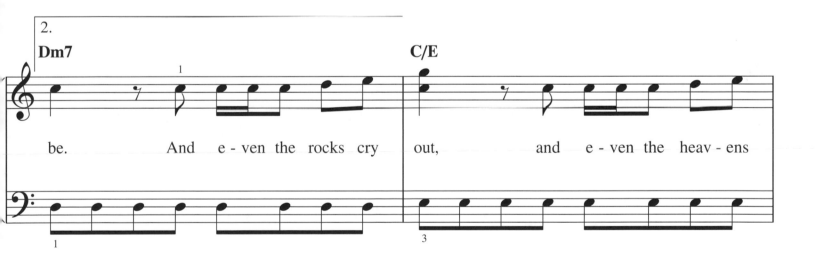

2.

Dm7

C/E

be.   And   e - ven the rocks cry   out,   and   e - ven the heav - ens

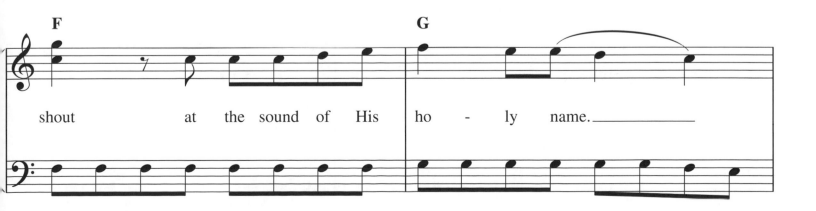

F

G

shout   at   the   sound of   His   ho - ly   name._____

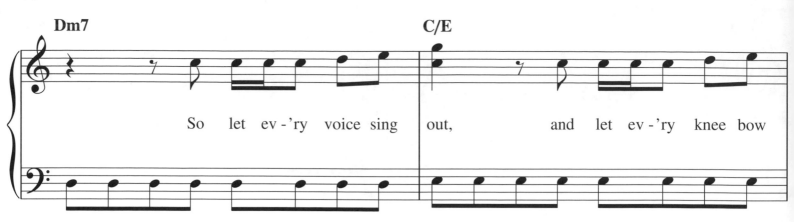

Dm7 / **C/E**

So let ev-'ry voice sing out, and let ev-'ry knee bow

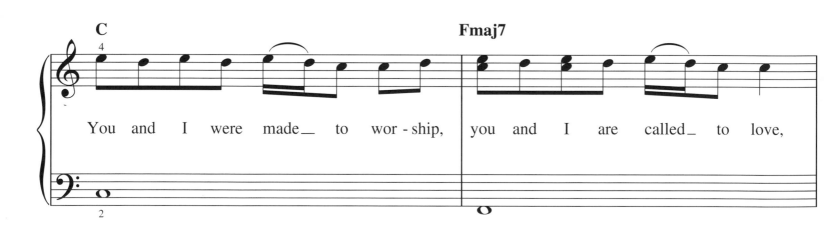

F / **G**

down; He is wor-thy of all our praise._____

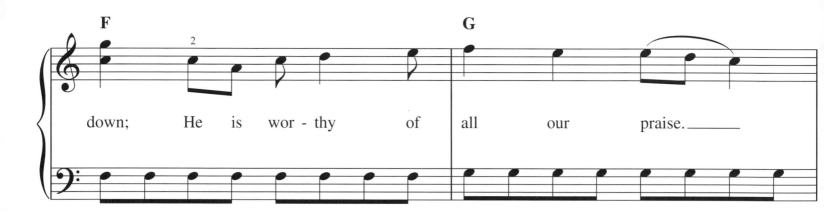

C / **Fmaj7**

You and I were made__ to wor-ship, you and I are called__ to love,

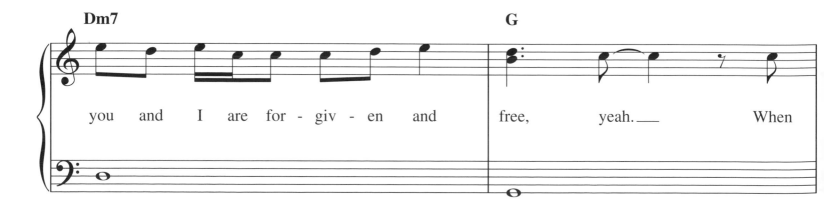

Dm7 / **G**

you and I are for-giv-en and free, yeah.__ When

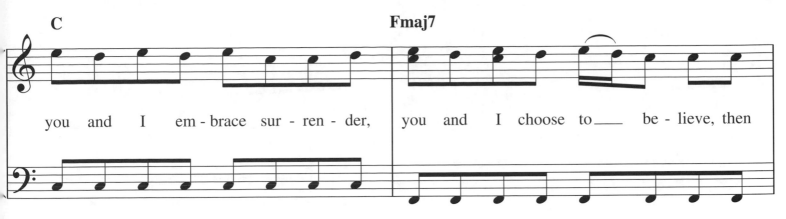

you and I em - brace sur - ren - der, you and I choose to___ be - lieve, then

you and I will see, you___ and I will see.

D.S. al Coda

be. Yeah,_____ we___ were meant to

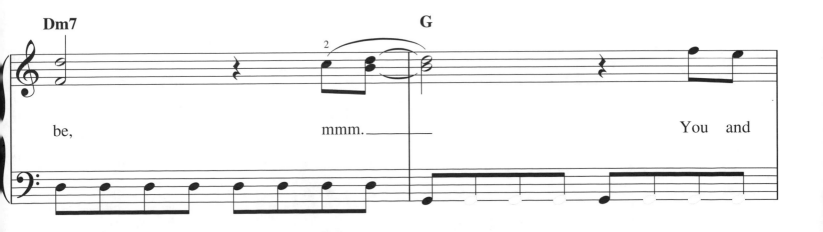

be, mmm._____ You and

I,_____ you and

yeah,_____

_____ yeah,_____ mmm,_____ and we were meant to

be.

LET GOD ARISE

Words and Music by CHRIS TOMLIN,
JESSE REEVES and ED CASH

wa - ters part___ be - fore us now.__
church will stand,_ she will en - dure.__

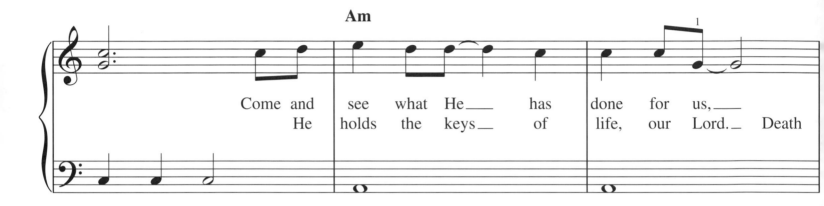

Am

Come and see what He__ has done for us,__ Death
He holds the keys__ of life, our Lord._ Death

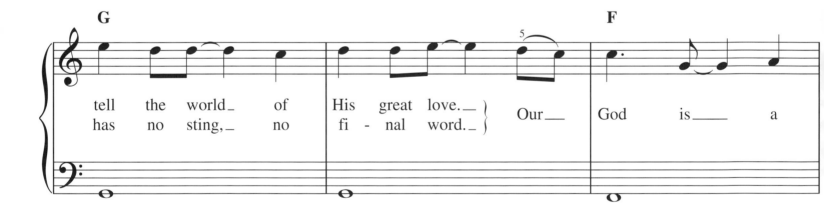

G   **F**

tell the world_ of His great love._ } Our__ God is___ a
has no sting,_ no fi - nal word._ }

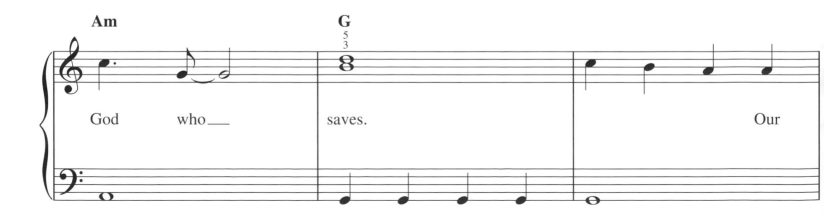

Am   **G**

God who__ saves.   Our

19

God is___ a God who___ saves.

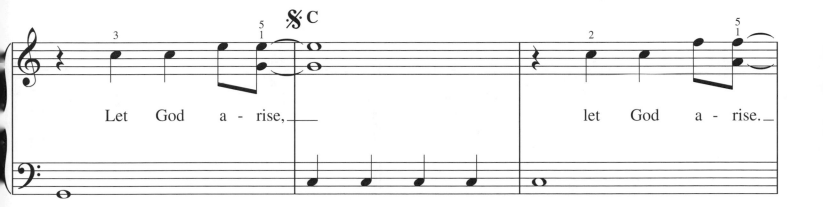

Let God a - rise,___ let God a - rise.___

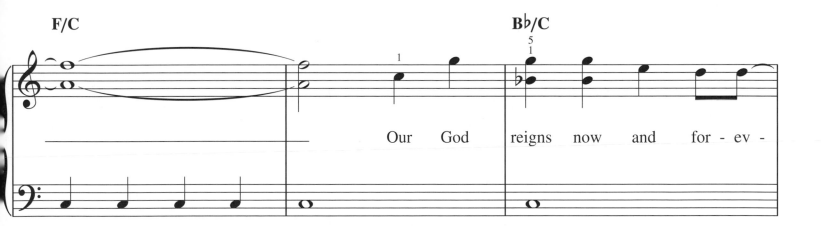

___ Our God reigns now and for - ev -

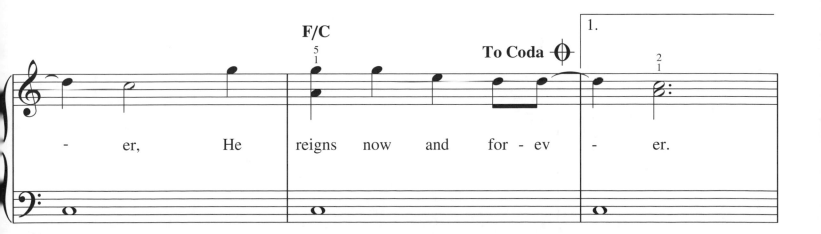

- er, He reigns now and for - ev - er.

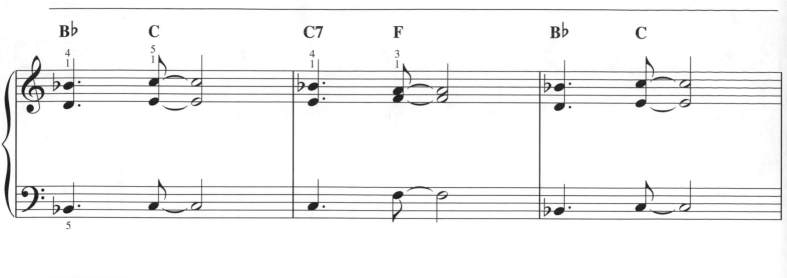

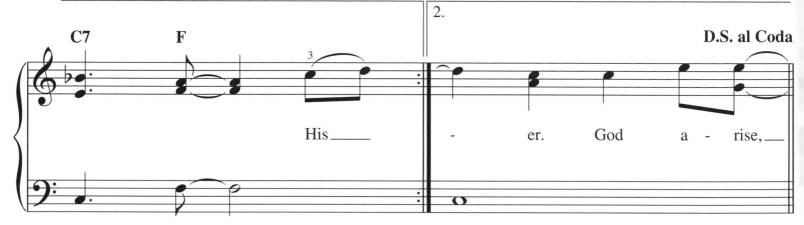

His_____ - er. God a - rise,____

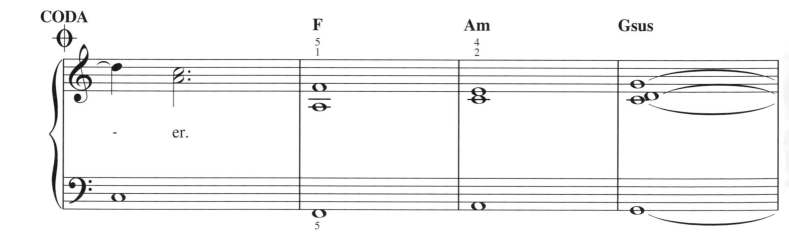

- er.

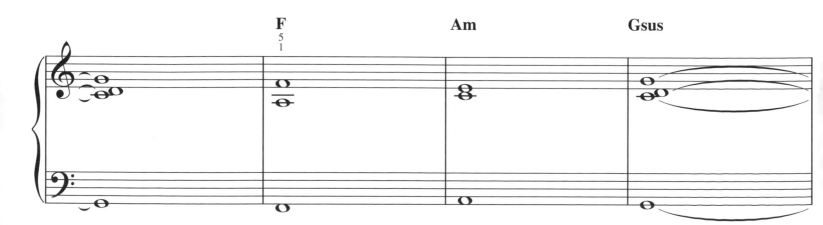

Our | God is____ a | God who____

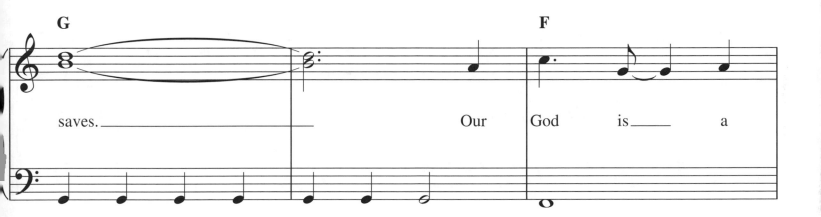

saves._____ | Our | God is____ a

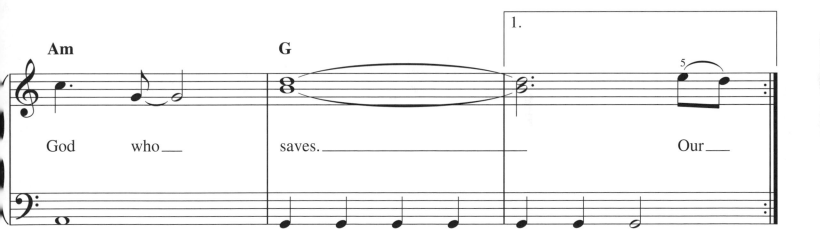

God who____ | saves._____ | Our____

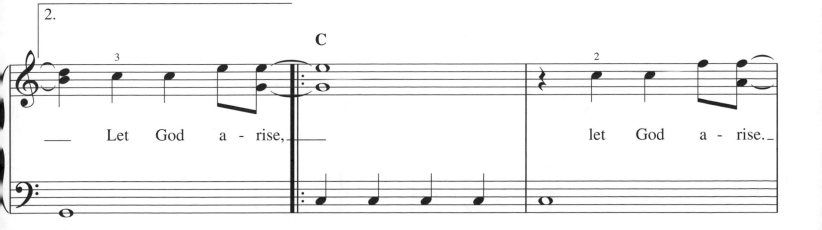

____ Let God a - rise,____ | let God a - rise.____

Our God reigns now and for-ev-

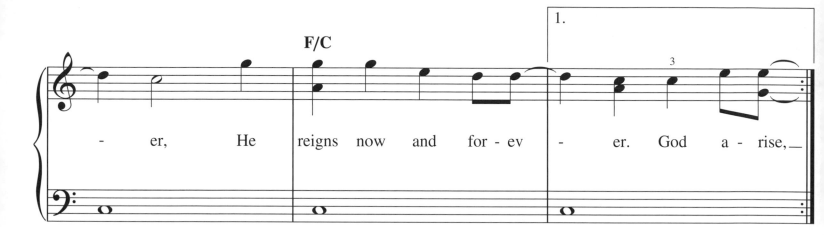

-er, He reigns now and for-ev - er. God a - rise,

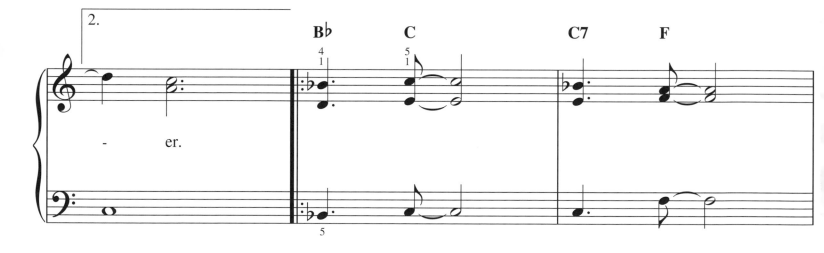

- er.

EVERLASTING GOD

Words and Music by BRENTON BROWN
and KEN RILEY

Moderate Rock

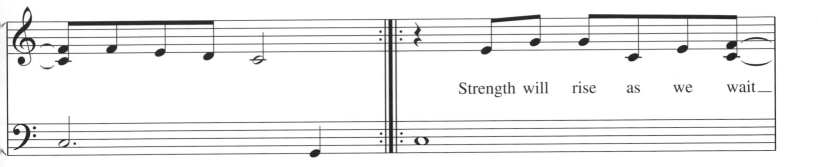

Strength will rise as we wait

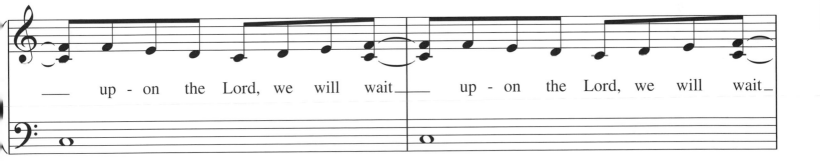

up - on the Lord, we will wait up - on the Lord, we will wait

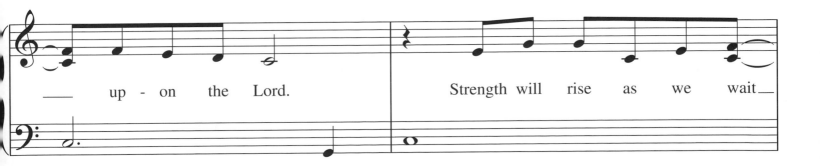

up - on the Lord. Strength will rise as we wait

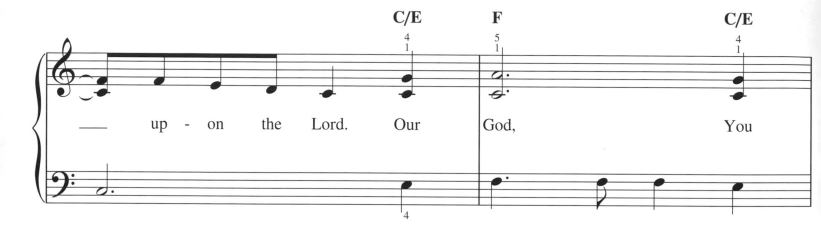

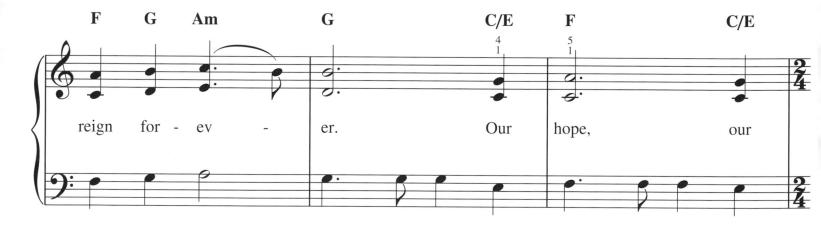

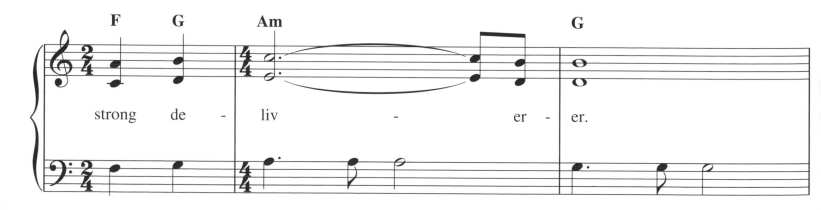

(1.,2.) You are___ the ev – er – last – ing God, the ev –
(D.S.) You're the___ de – fend – er of the weak, You com –

– er – last – ing God. You do___ not faint, You___
– fort those in need, You lift___ us up on___

won't grow wea – ry.___
wings like

wea – ry.___

26

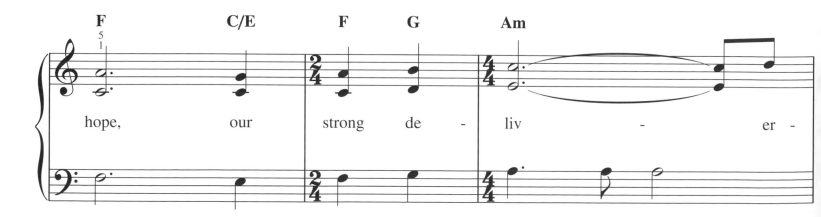

er.

G   **C**

You are___ the   ev - er - last - ing
You're the___ de - fend - er of   the

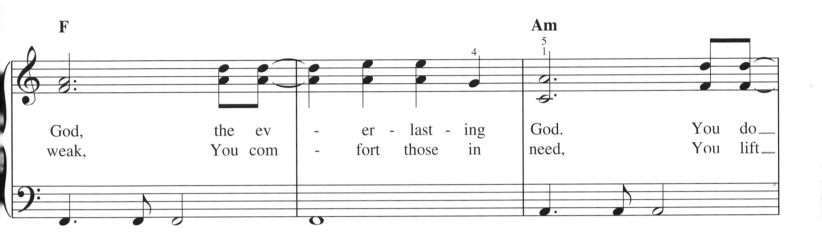

F   **Am**

God,   the ev   -   er - last - ing   God.   You do___
weak,   You com -   fort those   in   need,   You lift___

                                            F   **1.**

___ not faint, You___ won't   grow   wea - ry.___
___ us   up   on___ wings   like

2.   **C**

ea - gles.___   From___

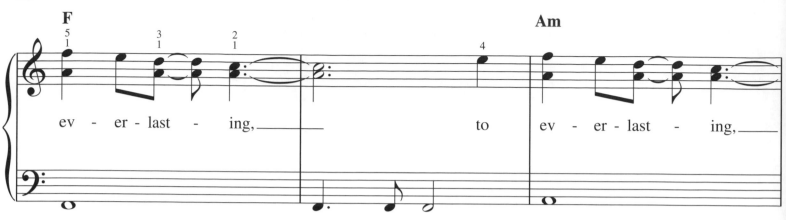

ev - er - last - ing,_____ to ev - er - last - ing,_____

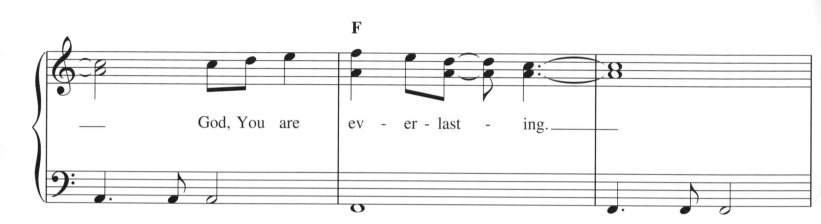

_____ God, You are ev - er - last - ing._____

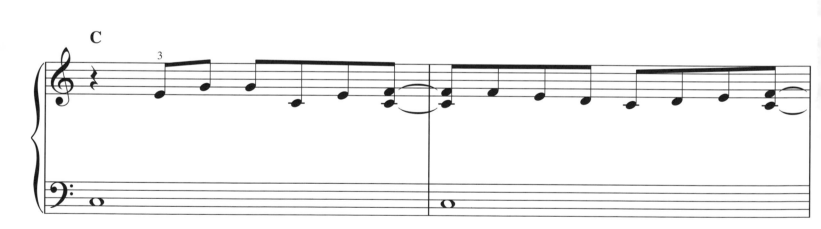

rit.

GLORY IN THE HIGHEST

Words and Music by CHRIS TOMLIN,
JESSE REEVES, DANIEL CARSON,
MATT REDMAN and ED CASH

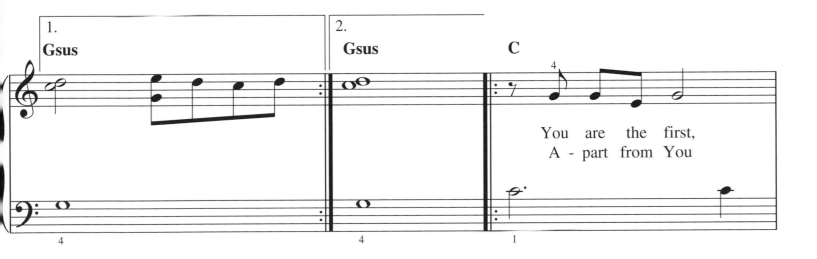

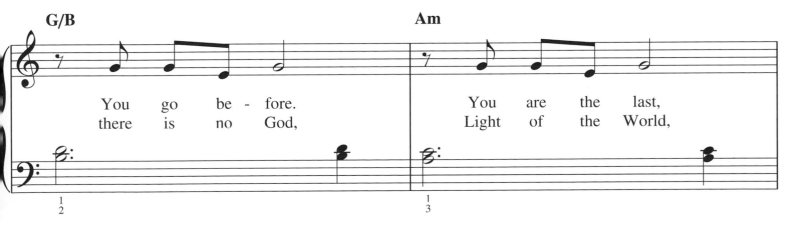

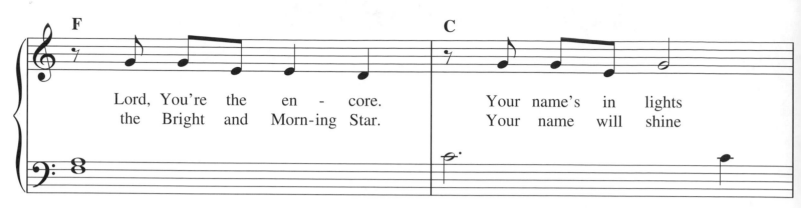

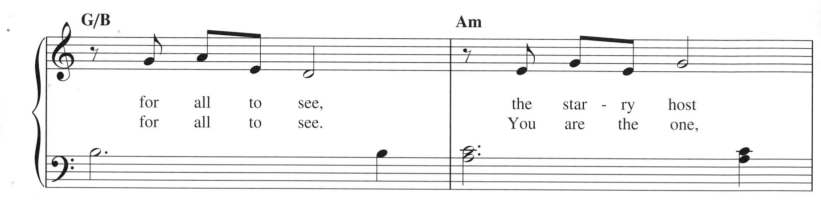

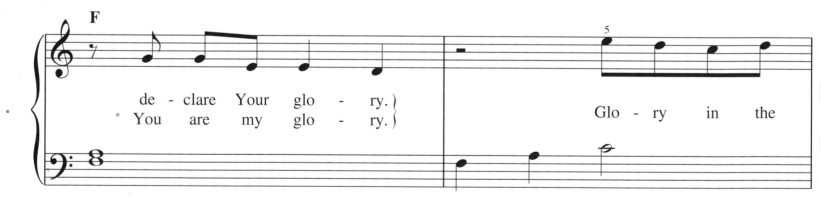

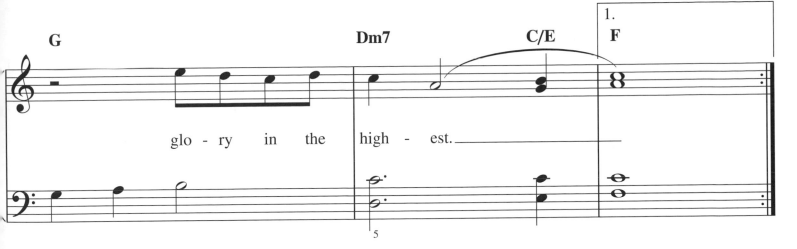

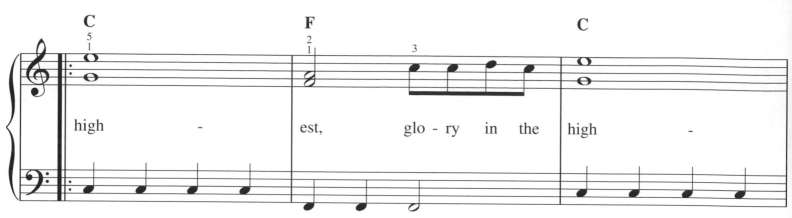

C **F** **C**

high - est, glo - ry in the high -

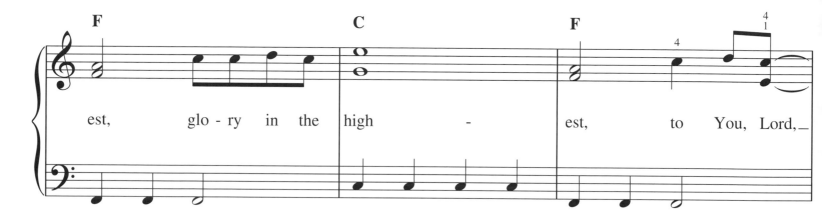

F **C** **F**

est, glo - ry in the high - est, to You, Lord,

C 1. **F** 2. **F**

to You, Lord. Glo - ry in the

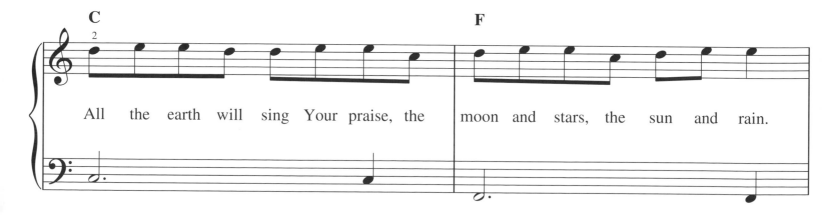

C **F**

All the earth will sing Your praise, the moon and stars, the sun and rain.

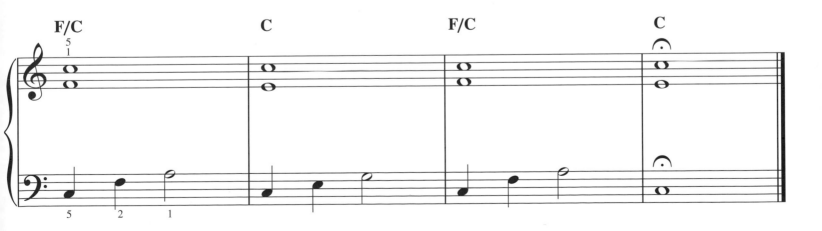

AWESOME IS THE LORD MOST HIGH

Words and Music by CHRIS TOMLIN,
JESSE REEVES, CARY PIERCE
and JON ABEL

Great are You, ___ Lord,
Where You send ___ us,

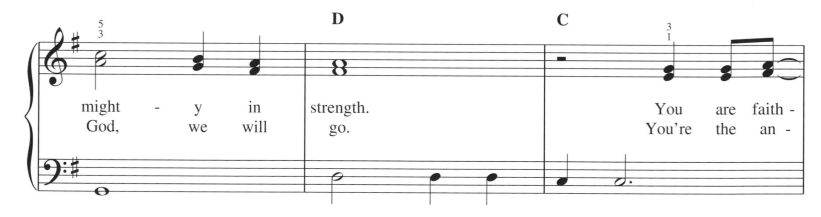

might - y in strength.
God, we will go.

You are faith-
You're the an -

- ful, _____ and You will ev - er be.
- swer, _____ we want the world __ to know.

We will praise_____ You all of our
We will trust_____ You when You call our

days.
name.

It's for Your glo - ry_____ we
Where You lead____ us,_____ we'll

of - fer ev - 'ry - thing.⎫
fol - low all____ the way.⎭

Raise your hands, all you na -

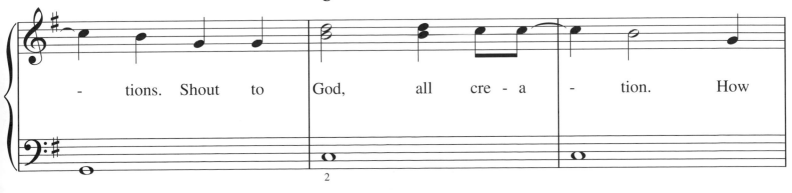

- tions. Shout to God, all cre - a - tion. How

36

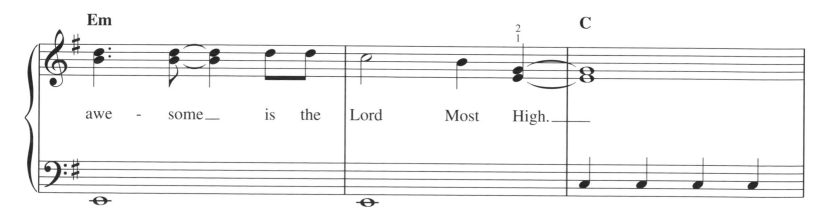

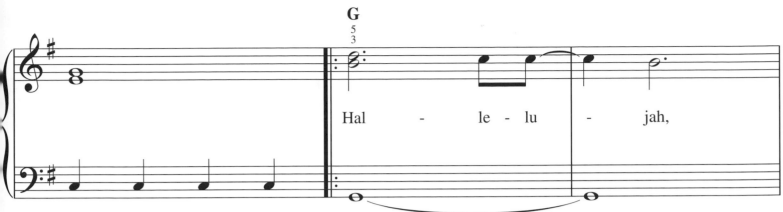

Hal - le - lu - jah,

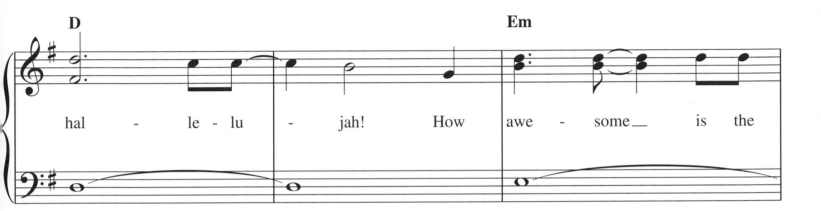

hal - le - lu - jah! How awe - some___ is the

Lord Most High.___

1.

2.

Raise your

hands, all you na - tions. Shout to God, all cre - a -

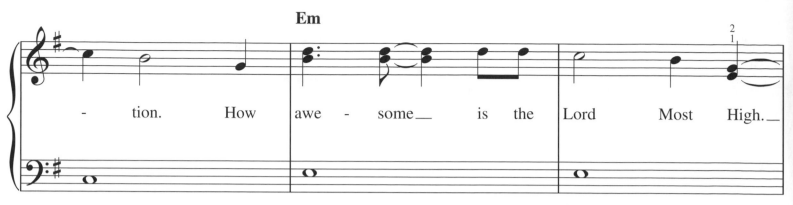

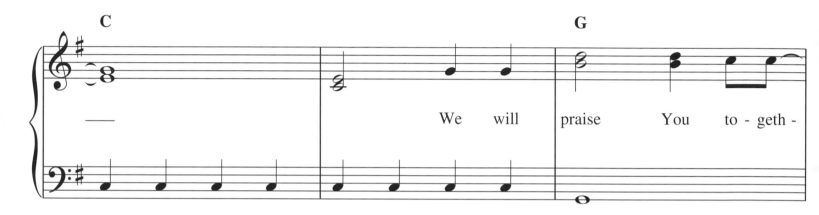

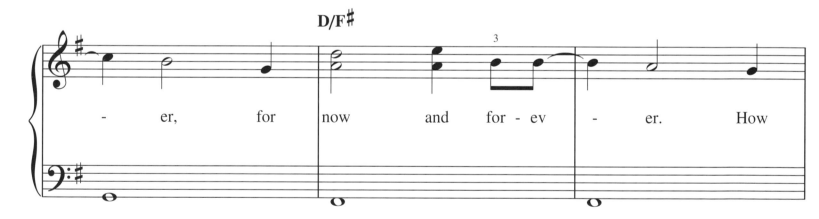

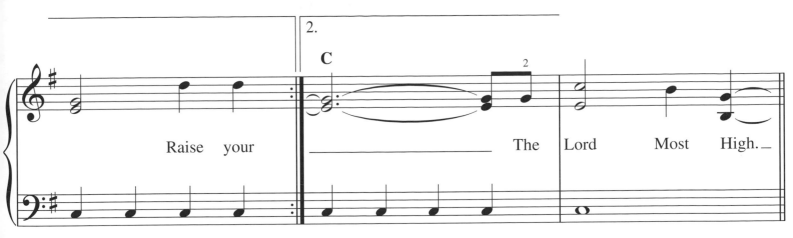

Raise your _____ The Lord Most High. _

How awe - some _ is the Lord Most High. _

GLORIOUS

Words and Music by CHRIS TOMLIN
and JESSE REEVES

We lift our

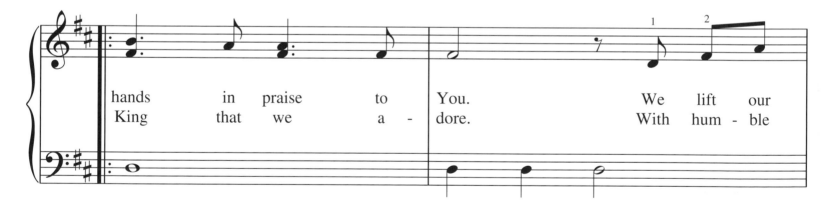

hands   in   praise   to   You.   We   lift   our
King   that   we   a - dore.   With hum - ble

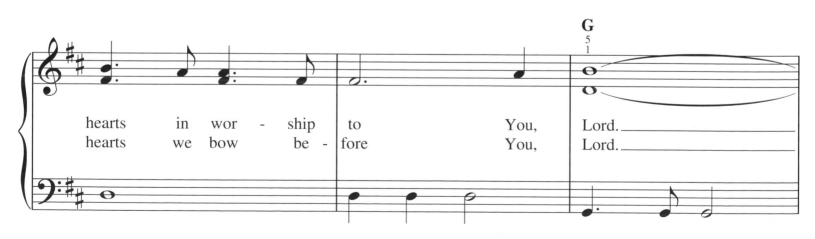

hearts   in   wor - ship   to   You,   Lord. _____
hearts   we   bow   be - fore   You,   Lord. _____

D

We lift our voice to You and
There is a place we long and to

sing, our great-est love will ev - er be You,
be. Face to face, we long to see You,

G   **D**

Lord, You, Lord. Glo - ri - ous,
Lord, You, Lord.

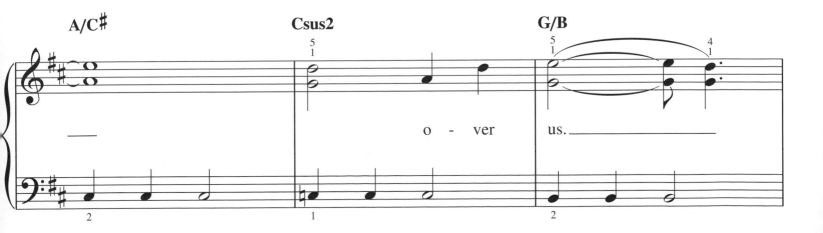

A/C♯   **Csus2**   **G/B**

o - ver us.

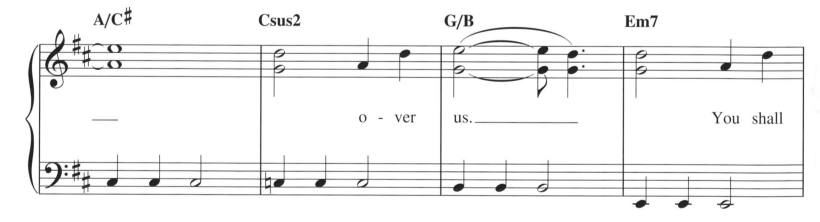

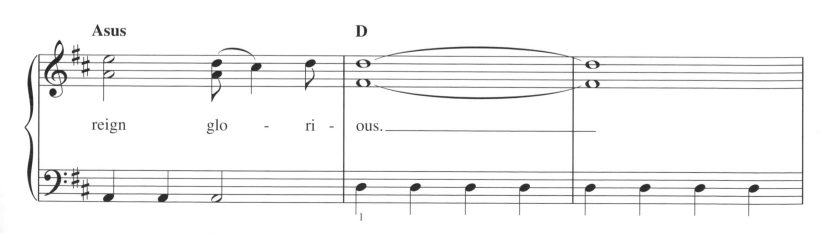

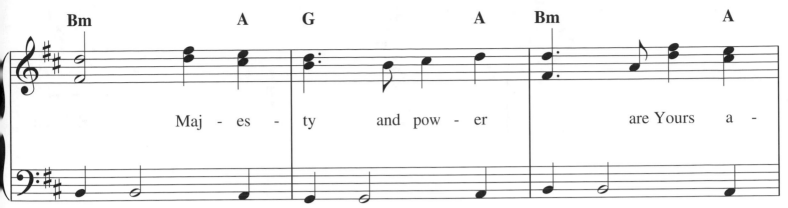

Maj - es - ty and pow - er are Yours a -

lone for - ev - er. Maj - es - ty and pow - er

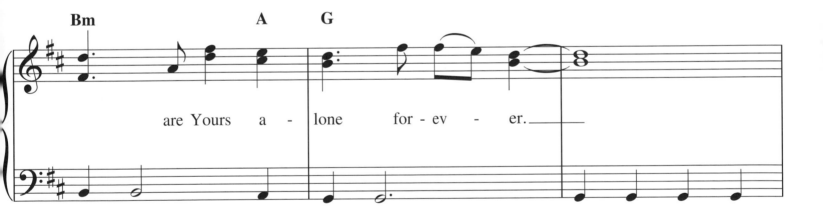

are Yours a - lone for - ev - er.

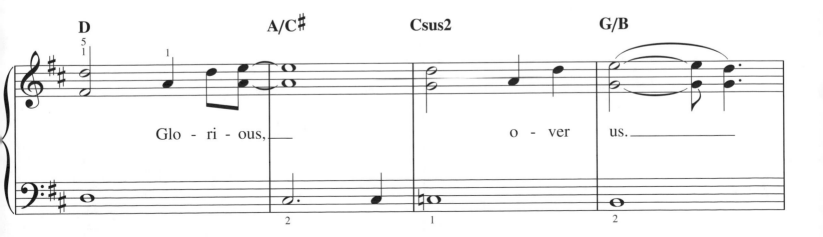

Glo - ri - ous, o - ver us.

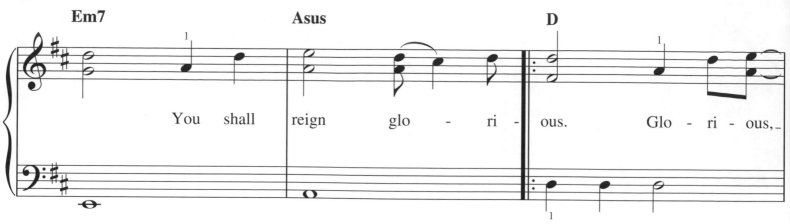

You shall reign glo - ri - ous. Glo - ri - ous,

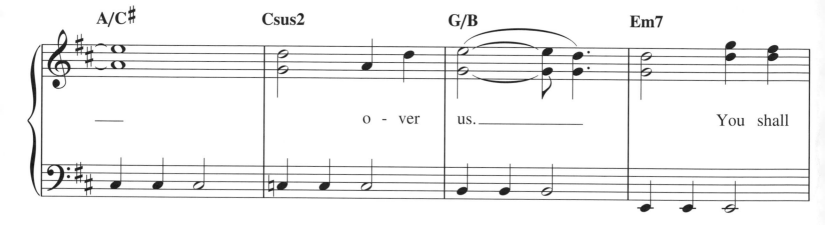

o - ver us. You shall

reign glo - ri - reign glo - ri - ous.

UNCREATED ONE

Words and Music by CHRIS TOMLIN
and J.D. WALT

Ho - ly Un - cre - at - ed One, Your
wor - thy Un - cre - at - ed One, from
Je - sus, Sav - ior, God's own Son,

beau - ty fills the skies. But the
heav - en to earth come down, You
ris - en, reign - ing Lord. Sus -

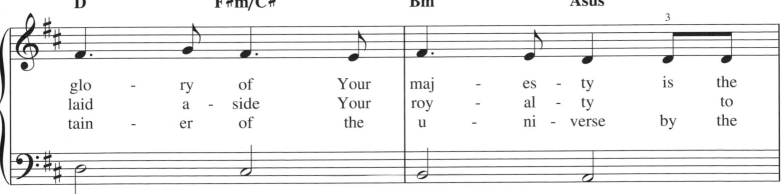

glo - ry of Your maj - es - ty is the
laid a - side Your roy - al - ty to
tain - er of the u - ni - verse by the

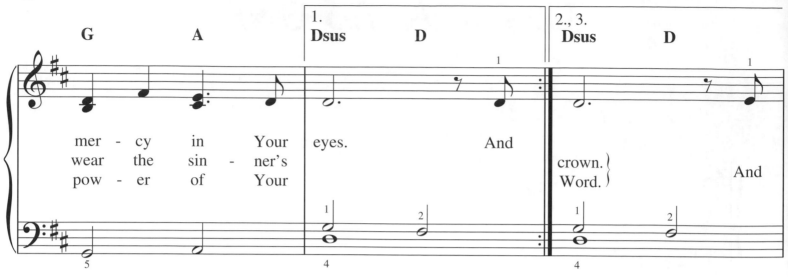

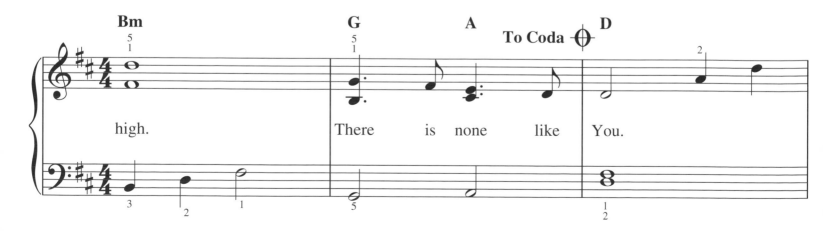

D.S. al Coda
(take 2nd ending)

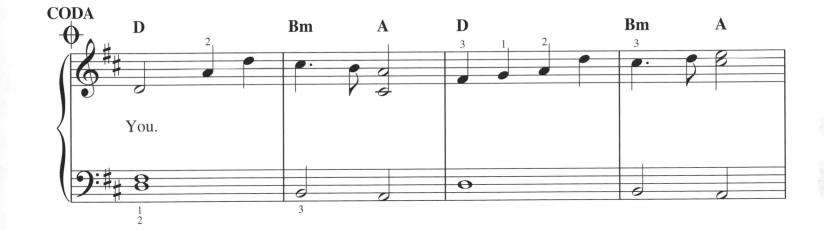

You.

And

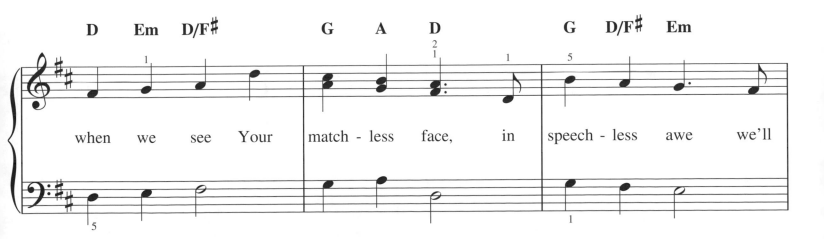

when we see Your match-less face, in speech-less awe we'll

48

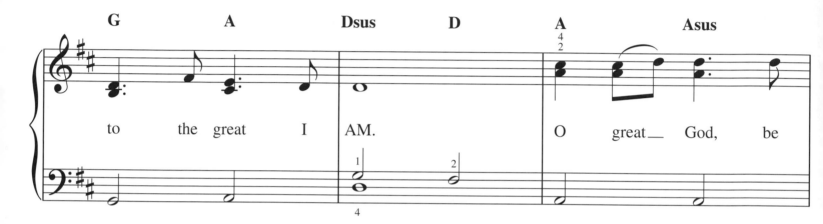

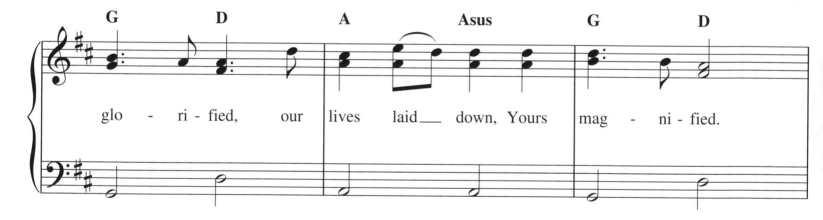

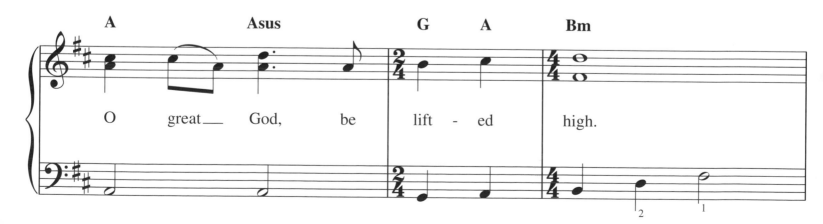

There   is   none   like   You,   there   is

none _____ like   You.

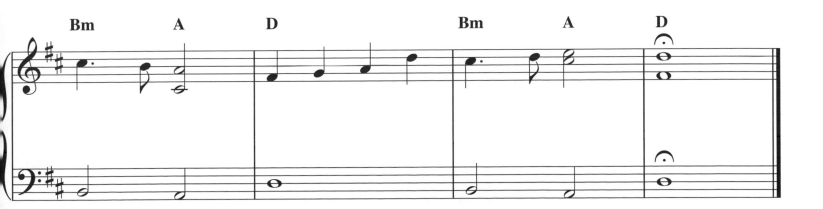

REJOICE

Words and Music by CHRIS TOMLIN,
JESSE REEVES and ED CASH

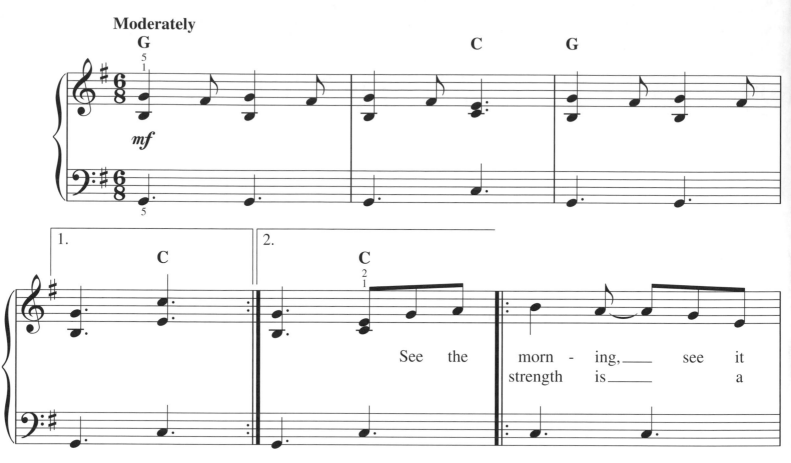

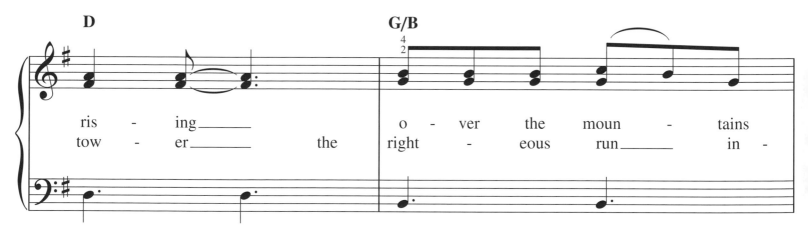

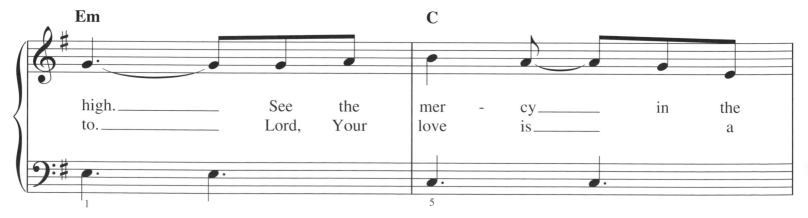

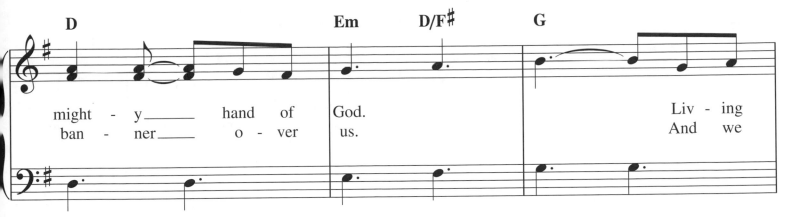

might - y_____ hand of God.
ban - ner_____ o - ver us.

Liv - ing
And we

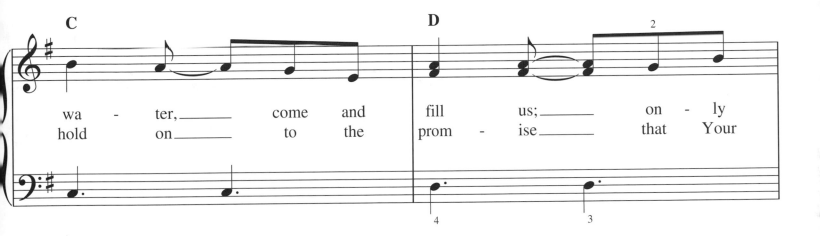

wa - ter,_____ come and fill us;_____ on - ly
hold on_____ to the prom - ise_____ that Your

You can sat - is - fy._____ Turn our sor - row_____ in - to
hold on us_____ is true._____ There's no oth - er_____ like You,

sing - ing_____ the song of_____ life._____ } Re -
Je - sus,_____ no one like_____ You._____

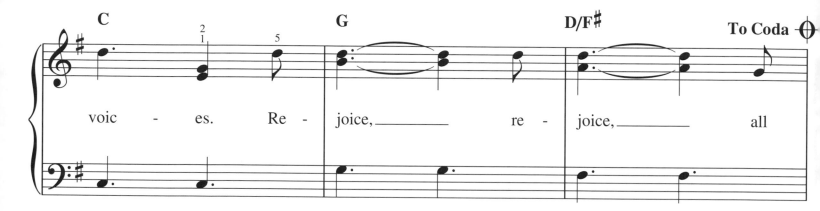

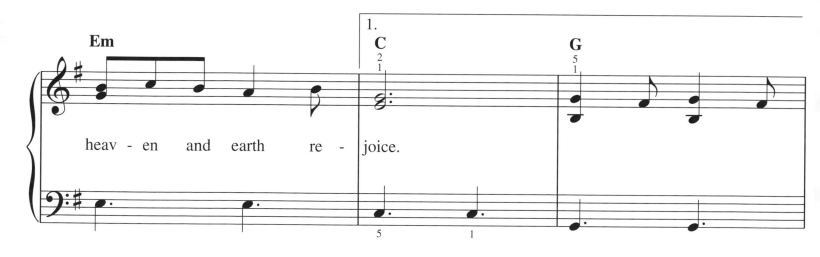

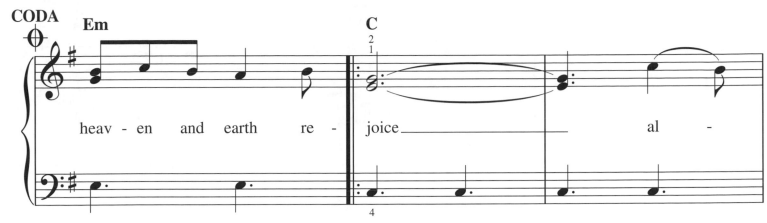

heav - en and earth re - joice_____ al -

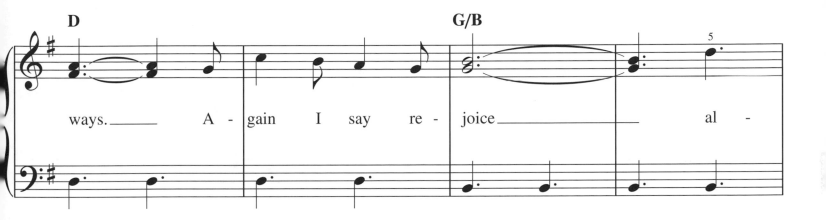

ways._____ A - gain I say re - joice_____ al -

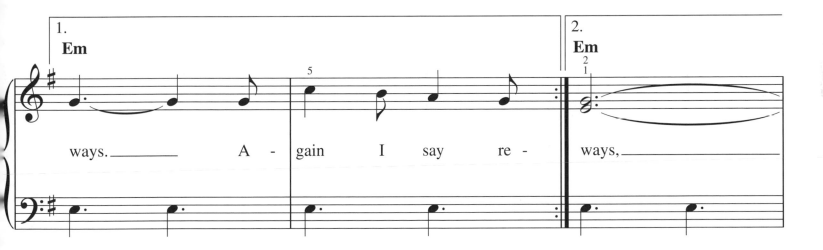

1.

ways._____ A - gain I say re -

2.

ways,_____

_____ al - ways._____ Re -

54

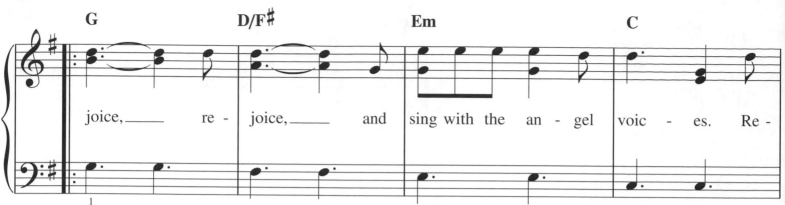

joice,_____ re - joice,_____ and sing with the an - gel voic - es. Re -

joice,_____ re - joice,_____ all heav - en and earth re -

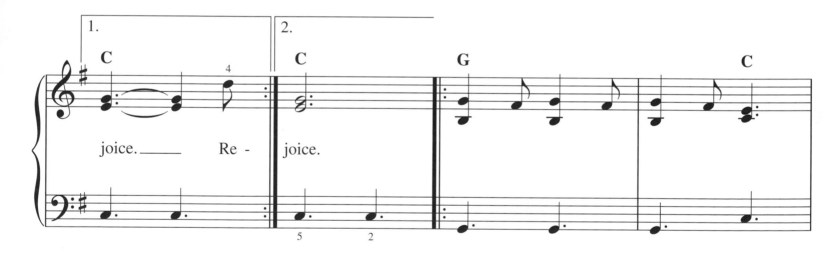

joice._____ Re - joice.

LET YOUR MERCY RAIN

Words and Music by CHRIS TOMLIN,
JESSE REEVES and ED CASH

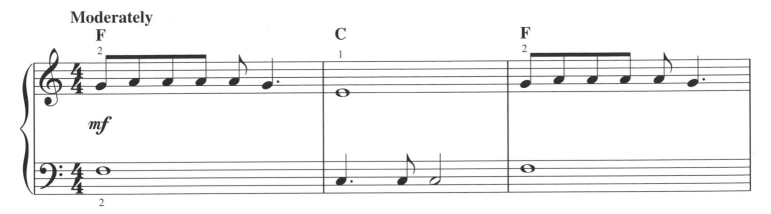

God, You have done__ great things. God,

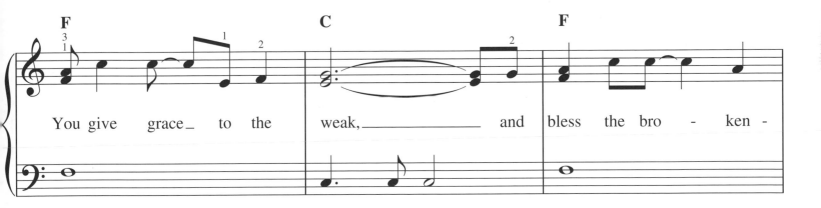

You give grace__ to the weak,_____ and bless the bro - ken -

heart - ed__ with a song of praise__ to sing.___ You reached

down and lift-ed us up. You came run-ning, look-ing for

us. And now there's noth-ing___ and no one be-yond Your

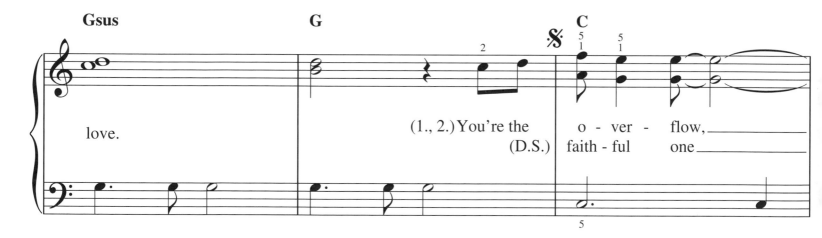

love. (1., 2.) You're the o-ver-flow,_____
(D.S.) faith-ful one_____

___ You're the foun-tain of___ my heart.⎰ So let Your
___ when the world's fall-ing___ a-part.⎱

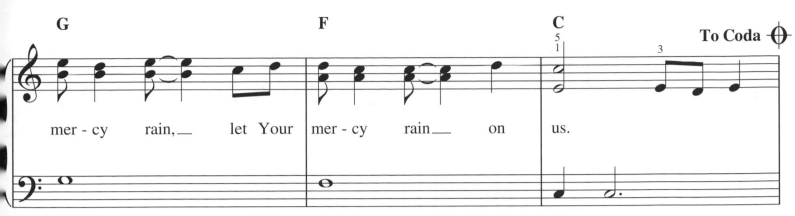

mer - cy rain,__ let Your mer - cy rain__ on us.

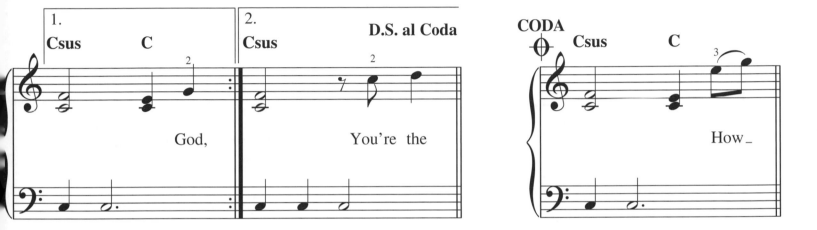

God,

You're the

How __

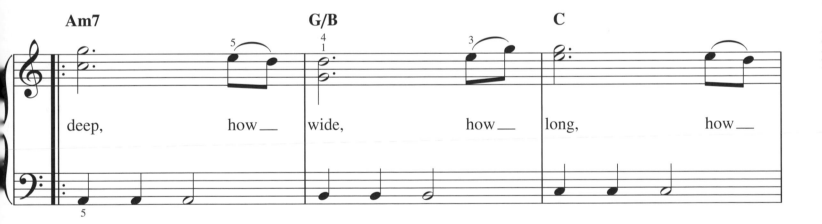

deep, how __ wide, how __ long, how __

high is Your love, is Your love. How __

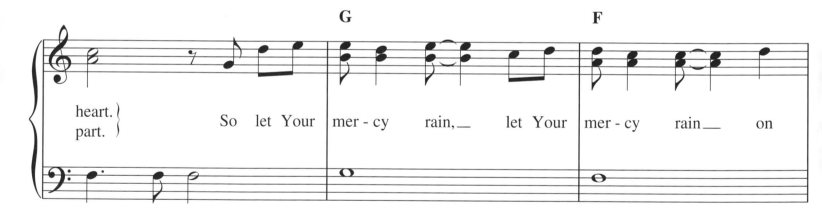

faith - ful   one _____   when my | world's fall - ing _____ a -

part.   So   let Your | mer-cy   rain, _   let Your | mer-cy   rain _____   on

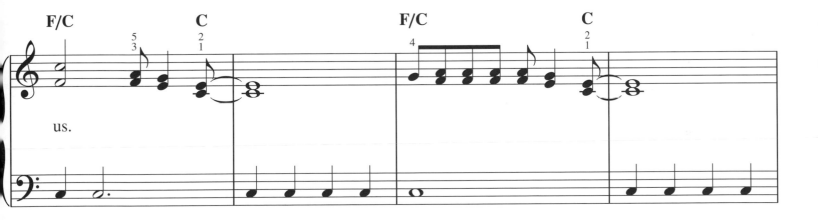

us.

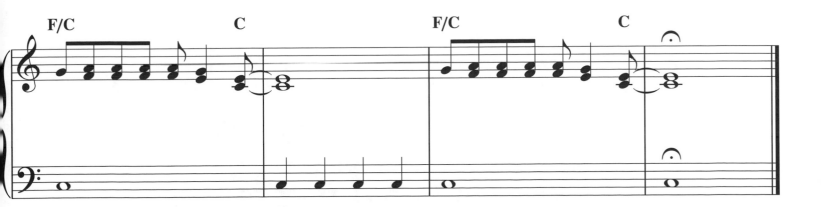

AMAZING GRACE
(My Chains Are Gone)

Words by JOHN NEWTON
Traditional American Melody
Additional Words and Music by CHRIS TOMLIN
and LOUIE GIGLIO

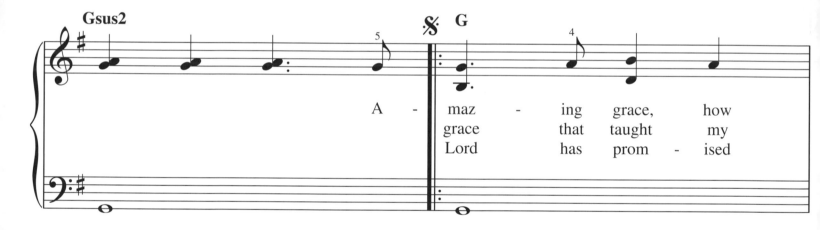

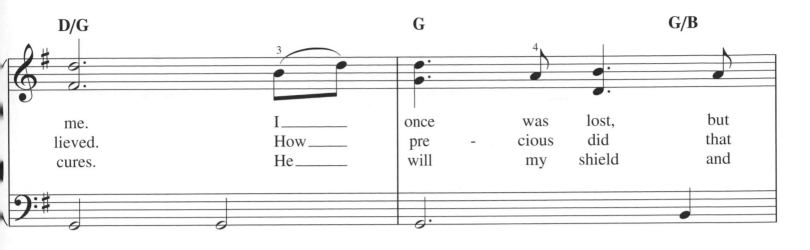

To Coda

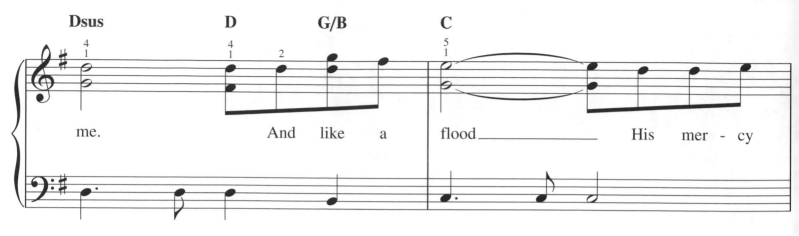

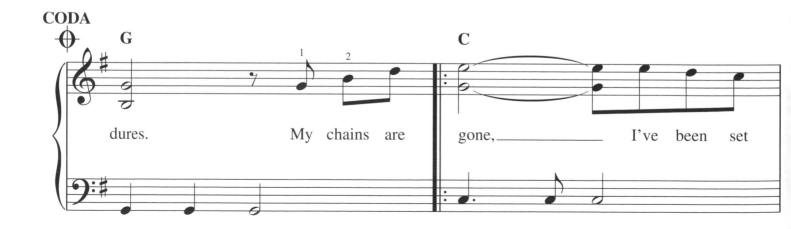

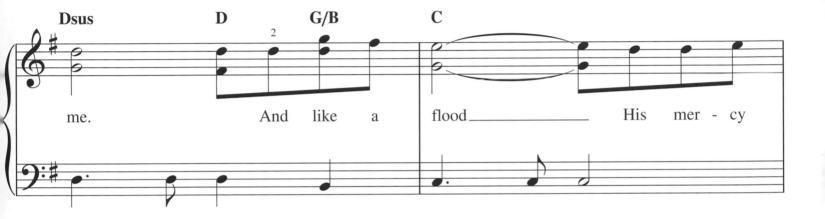

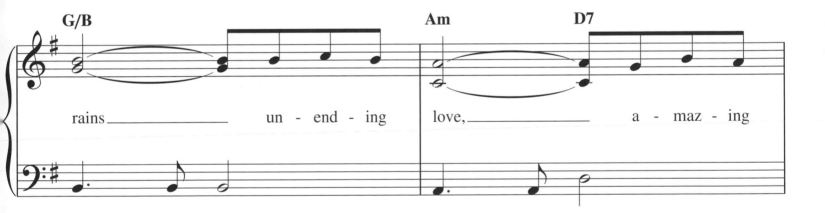

earth shall soon dis - solve like snow, the sun for - bear to

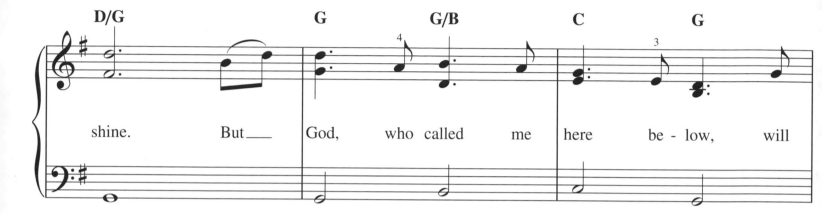

shine. But___ God, who called me here be - low, will

be for - ev - er mine, will be for - ev - er

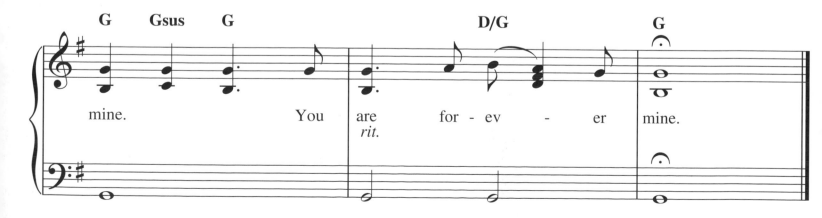

mine. You are for - ev - er mine.